Homes

Contents

Homes 2

Houses 4

Flats 6

Bungalows 8

Different homes 10

Index 12

Homes

house

mobile home

People live in lots of different types of homes.

Houses

How are these houses the same?

Flats

How are these flats the same?

Bungalows

How are these bungalows the same?

Different homes

bungalow

How are these homes different?

house-boat

flat

house

Index

 bungalow 8, 10

 flat 6, 11

 house-boat 3, 11

 house 4, 11

 mobile home 2

 oast-house 3